The Hermit

By

Pat Birtwistle

Cover illustration by

Taralynn Disher

ISBN 978-0-9947326-0-6

Patnor Publishing

In Loving Memory of

Norm Birtwistle

1943-2009

Chapter One

Preface

It was said that he lived in the bush near the lake. No one could tell much about him or had ever met him. Some said that they had seen him by the lake getting water. Others said that they saw someone going down the paths that were cut out in the bush. No one knew more than that.

The story was told that a man came back to these parts from the war. Things in war time can be bad for some men.

When he came home from that war he could not fit in. He did try, but then gave up and went into the bush. He liked it there.

The man had not hurt anyone **yet**, so the town just let him be. But that was about to come to an end.

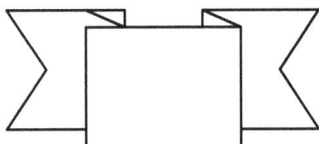

The bell rang and the kids ran for home. They had wanted to get out of school because this was the day they had been looking forward to for a long time. They had a camping trip planned. All their stuff was packed. They would camp all week-end. Beth and Kim would be in one tent. They had set up the tent in Kim's back yard. They set it up and took it down many times. The girls did not want the boys to get the best of them when it came time to set up.

Dan and Bob would be in another tent. Nick had a little tent so he would sleep in it.

The kids had picked out a good spot to camp. That spot was next to a lake. It was way up on a hill so they could see a lot from up there. There was a bush near the spot so that they could be out of the wind if it got too windy.

The kids had looked at a lot of spots before they found this one. The plan was that they would all get there after school and set up the tents.

After they had the tents up, they planned to explore. There were a lot of new things out there. There was the bush and then there was the lake with all the rocks along the edge. Beth said she would not like exploring. She would be happy just to be at the camp.

The kids all got to the camping spot at about the same time. They dragged their tents and backpacks up the hill and began to unpack.

"Do you think we forgot anything?" asked Nick.

"Are you kidding?" said Dan. "My mom asked if we were running away because I was packing so much."

"That's funny! My mom said the same thing," said Beth.

"If we kept to the list, we should be okay," Kim said.

The girls had no trouble setting up. Their tent was up in a flash. The boys did not get on so well. Nick had his up next. They all had to help Dan and Bob. The boys felt a little badly that the girls were helping them. No one said much but Kim and Beth felt good about it.

"Let's get what we need for the fire pit and camp fire then we can explore," said Bob.

There were lots of things for the fire just on the ground by the camp. It did not take them long to make a fire pit.

"It will soon be dusk," Nick said. "Let's go into the bush now. We do not want to be out there after the sun goes down."

"Why not?" asked Kim. "Are you afraid?" The kids all looked at Nick and laughed.

"Yes", Nick said. "I'm afraid of a lot of things, like snakes and runaway horses. Stuff like that." Now the kids were thinking back to all the times that they had been in trouble. They did not want trouble on this trip but...

Into the bush they went. Dan led the way.

"What do you think we'll find?" he asked.

"I hope not trouble!" Beth said.

"We don't get into trouble, Beth!" Bob said and the kids all laughed again.

They could not go too fast because of all the things on the ground. There were trees down and big rocks.

"Don't trip," Dan yelled back to the others.

"Do you think there are snakes out here?" Kim asked.

"Well, the lake is here so I would think there are," Bob said.

"It is beautiful here," Beth said. "And, I like the smell of the air."

As the boys pushed their way into the bush, they kept kicking stuff out of their way to make a path. That way they could find their way back up to camp.

Before the kids could think, a raccoon was in their way. It let out a cry and hit out at Bob. The kids stopped. They kept still. Beth was thinking she would be sick. No one said a thing. Then after a long, long time, the raccoon began to work its way to the lake. It was dusk and that is when raccoons look for food. After it left, the kids slowly left, too. They went up the path they had made.

"Now, that was not funny," said Nick. "I must say that I was afraid of that thing. Raccoons can be killers if they think they are trapped."

"I must say that I wasn't afraid," said Beth. At that, the kids all laughed a long time. They were making their way slowly up the path when Dan looked up into the trees.

"Look at those cobwebs," he said. "Have a look at that one." With the setting sun they could see the cobwebs. They looked beautiful.

"If the cobwebs are that big, how big must the spiders be?" asked Beth.

At that, the girls began to go faster up the path.

Then the boys saw that the girls had stopped. Kim was down looking at something on the ground.

"What do you think they are doing?" asked Bob.

"They are picking something but I can't think of what it could be out here," Nick said.

When the boys got to the spot, they could see that Kim and Beth were picking something up and eating it.

"What are you two doing?" asked Nick. "You can't be eating those things, are you? You'll get sick. You could die!"

"We just wanted a little food," said Beth. "And, there they were, all these little red things. They are sooooo good. Want some?"

"Are you nuts?" Bob said trying to see the things in Kim's hand. Dan was looking at them in Beth's hand. The two girls began laughing.

"We just wanted to play a little trick on you," Kim said. "We saw them and just let on that we were eating. The trick worked. Just look at you!"

The girls kidded them all the way back to the camp. Soon, the guys were laughing too. The wind was getting up and the sun had set. The kids lit the campfire.

"It's a good thing we had this all set up to go before we left," Dan said. "It's too black out now to be looking for wood to make a fire."

The kids all began getting food from their backpacks and talking all at once.

"Here are the cans that were on the list."

"I've got all this stuff my mom put in."

"I have a lot more, too, because mom packed mine."

"What are we going to do with all this food? There is way too much for us."

"Are you kidding?" asked Nick. "I could eat a horse."

After eating the kids put the rest of the food away and sat by the fire for a long time. Now it was time for the guys to get back at Beth and Kim for playing a trick on them.

"What kinds of things do you think are out in the bush after the sun sets?" asked Dan.

The girls were getting a little upset but they did not want to let on.

"Do you think there are bears in this bush?" asked Bob.

"Well, if there are raccoons there must be bears. Skunks come out to look for food after dark," said Bob.

"Will you stop it!" said Beth. "You are just trying to get us upset because we tricked you. We are not going to let you get to us. Are we Kim?"

"You said it. And I think it's time we got some sleep. I, for one, could go to sleep right here and I don't want to do that. Should we let the fire just go out or should we put it out?" asked Kim.

"Let's just let it go," Nick said.

The kids went to their tents and got into their sleeping bags. They were yelling and laughing. They did not want the day to end but they were sleepy.

"We had a day without trouble and it is so much fun camping out here," one yelled.

"I think we are past getting into trouble."

"We have Dan with us, so we will have some trouble before the week-end is over," Nick laughed from his tent.

"I'll get you for that one," Dan yelled back.

They began to get sleepy and the yelling stopped.

Bob was still not sleepy so he lay in the dark thinking. The rest of the kids were nodding off when Dan let out a "VROOM".

"Oh Dan" yelled Bob. "What a smell!" The kids all laughed and laughed until they all had nodded off at last.

The camp was dark and quiet. Then something made Nick sit up in his tent. He sat quietly. He could not think of what had made him wake up like that. It was dark and he could not see a thing but something told him that there was something or someone by the fire pit. He did not want to yell to the rest of the kids.

There it was again! Something was going past his tent. He could tell that it had been next to Kim and Beth's tent and was going back that way. He sat quietly for a long time. He could not think of what he should do.

Should he try to see what was out there or just keep quiet and let it go away?

Chapter Two

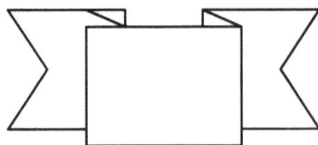

By the time the guys began to get up, the girls were getting the food from their backpacks. Dan came out of their tent. Nick was the last one up.

"Why do you look like you had no sleep, Nick?" Beth asked.

"Did you all sleep okay?" Nick asked. "There was something or someone out here last night. It was quiet but it was here."

The rest of the kids gave him an odd look. They had a good night's sleep and were thinking that Nick was just making this up so that they would be afraid.

"I didn't hear a thing," Beth said. "You are just making that up."

"No, someone or something was here. I sat up for a long time. At last it left but it was here."

"Okay. So let's eat and get going. There is so much to see and do," said Dan not looking at Nick.

By now the food was hot and they ate. After eating they put the food and cooking things away. Then they set up the fire pit for night.

"Let's take some food with us." Kim said. "That way we will not have to come back before dusk."

Nick said, "I think we should come back at noon. We should check on the camp. If something is after this stuff and we are away too long, we could be in big trouble."

They all said they would come back just to keep Nick happy. They headed out to the hill of rocks that ran along the lake. They helped one another over the rocks and were doing well. Just then Dan spotted someone by the water.

"Look down there!" he said. "What is that man doing?"

"I can't tell from up here," said Bob, "but it looks as if he is looking for something in the water. What could he be looking for away out here? Let's go down and find out."

"No way!" said Kim. "Look down! We could not make it down. And if we did, we would not make it back up."

"We have lots of time before noon. Maybe we could help him find what he is looking for. It could be a lot of fun." Bob said.

Nick did not say a thing. He was thinking of that thing in the night that was at their camp. Maybe the man down by the water was at the camp. Maybe he was trying to get them down there.

"Kim thinks you guys are crazy," Beth said. "And, so do I. That is a lot of rock to get over just to get down there. Then, how do we get back up?"

By now, Bob and Dan began to make their way down to the water. The others were afraid of what trouble they could be in if they all went down so they held their ground. They were not going.

On the way down to the water Bob and Dan could not think why Nick had not come with them.

"It is not like Nick to be afraid." Dan said. "He could make it down these rocks better than we can."

"Something has gotten into him. When we got up he looked badly and he did not say much. Maybe we will see what we can get out of him at noon," Bob said.

"OW!" yelled Dan. He looked down at his hand and saw blood. There was blood on the rock, too. He let out another cry and let go. Bob grabbed him just as he fell.

"Grab on Dan!" Bob yelled. "I can't keep you up! Grab on to something."

Dan's hand was badly hurt. Bob could not tell how bad it was, but he could see all the blood. He looked down. The man was in the water but did not look up when Dan yelled. The wind from the lake had kept the yell from getting down that far. Then Bob looked up the hill.

The other kids could tell that something had stopped Dan and Bob but they could not see the blood.

They were thinking that the two guys had stopped to have a little rest. They could see Bob hugging the rock next to him.

"Dan, get that hand up," said Bob. "You don't want to shed too much blood. Now, find a good spot on the edge of that rock as I let you down. Good! Good! Now, let go of me slowly. There you are. Whew."

Dan sat down with his one hand up. The blood was slowing down now. As Bob came over and sat next to Dan he asked "Are you okay?"

"Yeah, but now what?" he asked. "I don't think I can make it up or down."

"You can't, but I can," Bob said. "Do I go up to the others or down and try to get that man to help us?"

"I don't think the rest of the kids could be much help," said Dan. "I think we should ask that guy. He may say no, but I think it will be our best shot to get me out of this mess."

Bob began making his way down the rocks. He was going slowly. He did not want to get into trouble on his way down. He was not thinking of what he would say to the man when he got down there. He just wanted to get to the ground and then he would think of what he would say.

Nick, Beth and Kim were looking at Dan sitting on a rock and Bob going down the hill.

"What do you think that is all about?" Kim asked.

"Dan does not like to let others win. He would not let Bob go down if there was not some trouble," said Beth.

"I should be down there with them", Nick was thinking. "They are not that good at things like this."

"I told them there would be trouble if they went down there," Beth said. "Now we can't do much to help. We don't know what kind of mess they are in."

"If we are going to help we will have to get some rope," said Nick. "There is some in my tent back at the camp. You two stay here. I'll get it."

"We have some in our tent as well," Kim said. "Maybe you should get it, too. We may need a lot and we do not want to have to go all the way back to get more."

Bob got over the last of the rocks. He felt good to be on the ground. When he looked up, he saw that Dan was still in the same spot. He headed over to where the man was. The man had a rod in his hand. As Bob came up to him, the man looked up.

"Hi," Bob yelled.

"What are you doing here, kid?" the man asked. He looked cross.

"I need a hand," Bob said. "See that kid up there on the rocks? He is hurt and cannot get up or down without help. Would you give us a hand?"

"Can't you see that I have other things to do?" the man said. "You kids should not be out here and you should not be on those rocks. This is no place for kids. So get lost!"

Bob had not met a man like this guy. He wanted to get out of there but Dan had to get help and so he asked, "Could you just come and help me get him down and then we won't bug you again?"

"It would be best if you left NOW, kid," the man said. "You don't want to make me mad and I am just about to get mad. Now get lost!"

Bob took one last look at the man. He was about to say something when the man yelled, "GET OUT OF HERE! NOW!"

Bob began backing up. He was afraid that the man was going to hit him with the rod. He kept backing up as the man was waving the rod at him. Bob fell and the man came at him still waving the rod in the air. Bob got up before the man could get to him. Then Bob made a run for it. He knew the man was after him so he ran into the bush. Without looking back he felt that the man was right behind him waving the rod like crazy. After running for a long time he stopped, looked back and saw that he was alone. He sat down.

"Now, what should I do?" he began thinking.

Bob wanted to go back the way he had come down, but he was afraid of the man. He sat quietly and began to plan what to do next. Back to the camp? Back to find the others? Or what?

Chapter Three

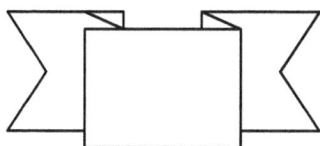

Dan sat looking down as Bob went up to the man. "I hope this guy will help us out," he was thinking. Then he saw the man move and try to hit Bob with the rod. When he saw that, he got up and was going to try to make it down the rocks to help. He fell back. He knew that there was no way he could help. He looked up to yell for Nick. All he could see were Beth and Kim – no Nick. He saw Bob take off running with the man after him. The man was running fast but then he stopped. Bob kept running. At last he could not see Bob and the man went back to his spot by the water.

"What a mess," Dan said to himself. "Beth was right. This is crazy. We should not have come down here. Now I can't tell where Bob is. I hope he can find his way back."

When Nick got to the camp, he was dripping wet. He sat down. After a little time he got back up and went to get some water. After that he went to the girls' tent but could not find the rope. As he was about to give up, he saw something at the edge of Kim's sleeping bag. It was the rope.

He grabbed it and ran to his tent. Grabbing some more water and more rope he began running back to the spot where he had left Beth and Kim. On the way he was thinking of a plan to help Dan. How much trouble was Dan in? When he got to the girls they told him about the man. They were afraid that he may have hurt Bob with the rod he was waving in the air.

"You can tell me about all of that after we get Dan. Let's get him up here. Where's Bob?" asked Nick.

Kim was upset and said, "That's what we were telling you. Bob ran off with that man after him. We don't know where he is."

They had to think about who was in more trouble, Bob or Dan.

"Well, let's get Dan up here and then we'll think about Bob, okay?" said Nick.

Nick had the rope and tied one end around a big tree. He put the ends of the two ropes so that they would not let go. Then he said to the girls, "Which one of you is going down?"

Kim and Beth looked at Nick as if he were crazy.

"Don't look at me," said Kim. "I'm not going down there."

"Nick, you know I can't do it," Beth said. "I'm afraid just looking down at Dan. I know I will fall if I try. I just know it!"

Nick was getting upset now. He said, "One of you has to go down and help Dan. If I go, you two will not get us back up here. Beth, you will not be much help with the rope and you are too little. So, you will have to do down."

"I was thinking," said Kim. "Why not just let the rope down to Dan? He looks like he could make it if he had the rope. Let's try that and see if it works. Make a good loop for his feet at the end of the rope. That way, we can all help pull him up."

"Okay, let's try it. If it doesn't work, one of you will have to go down," said Nick.

Nick made a loop at the end of the rope for Dan's feet. He began letting that end of the rope down slowly to Dan. He did not want the rope to get stuck on rocks. If it did, he would have to go down after it.

Dan was looking up at the rope. He kept saying to himself, "Come on! Come on!" His hand hurt but not as badly as before. He knew that if the rope made it down to him, he could get back up to the top of the rocks. Then the rope got stuck on a rock.

"Oh no!" said Dan.

Nick gave the rope a big wave and it went out into the air. He began running it faster down the rocks. He felt that it went better that way.

When it got to Dan he grabbed the end. He put his feet into the loop. With his good hand he ran the rope around himself. Then he yelled up to the kids, "Okay, let's go!"

Nick, Beth and Kim ran their end of the rope around a big tree. When they saw that Dan was all set, they pulled the rope around the trunk as they dragged him up. Dan yelled, "All set!" and Nick said, "One, two, three PULL!" Dan came off the ground. "One, two, three PULL!" They were making their way around the tree trunk. They were dripping wet from the heat when Dan yelled out. Beth went to the edge to look.

"What?" she yelled down to him.

"I want a little rest on this rock. My ribs and hand hurt. I will be okay after a little rest."

Beth told the others, so they sat down to rest too.

When Dan yelled back up, "Okay", the kids got up and began pulling as they had before.

They were doing well but they knew that Dan was a long way down. Nick stopped pulling. The girls looked over at him. He was looking at the spot where the rope was on the edge of the rocks going down to Dan. There was one spot on the rope that was thin. If they were to try to pull it around the tree it could give way. They did not want to try pulling it, but could not think of what to do.

Dan was yelling, "Come on! Get me up!"

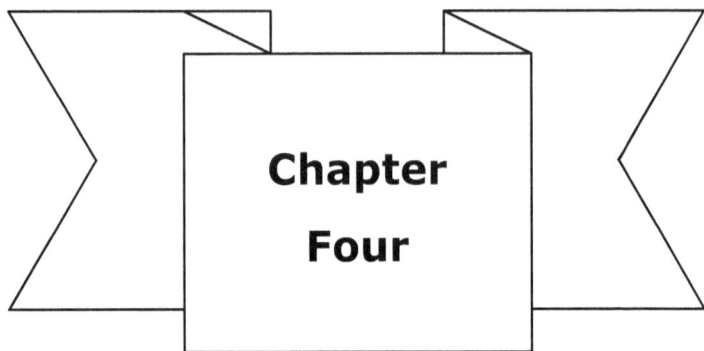

Chapter
Four

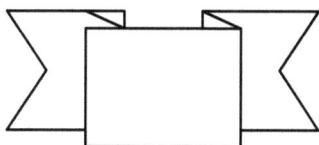

Beth was getting more and more upset at

Dan yelling. At last she went over to the edge and

yelled down to him.

"We have some trouble up here, so just stop

yelling. We're doing the best we can!" Then she

went back to Nick and Kim.

Dan stopped yelling but he did not know

how long he would last. The rope was hurting his

feet. His good hand felt funny as if it had died.

The other hand did not hurt as much but he knew

that if he were to try to use it, the blood would

begin again. The kids had been doing a good job getting him up. He could not think of what could have made them stop. He knew he should not yell up at them because Beth had been so upset, but this was getting to be too much.

At the top of the hill the kids were trying to think of ways they could get the thin spot on the rope past the tree trunk.

"You two pull on the part around the tree. I'll pull on the rope that goes down to Dan. We will have to do this slowly or the rope will snap and Dan will land on the rocks," said Nick.

They gave it a try but Nick could not get the rope over the edge of the rocks. So Kim went to help him and left Beth to pull the rope at the tree trunk.

"One, two, three, PULL!" Kim said.

They got Dan up a little more and the rope did not snap when Beth pulled it. After pulling two or three times, they stopped to rest.

"This is going to take too long," said Kim. "Do you think Dan will be okay if it takes us a long time?"

Nick was just going to say something but didn't. He backed up and went over to where Beth was resting. He let Kim see that he wanted to tell them something. Kim got up from her resting spot and the three of them went behind some rocks. When he thought they could not be seen, Nick stopped.

"When I looked up from the rope I saw something over there," said Nick. "I think it must have been someone who did not want us to see them because when I looked up again no one was there. We can't stop what we have to do to get Dan up, but just look out for trouble up here, too. Now let's get back to Dan."

By now, they were rested and wanted to get Dan up before he fell. They were trying not to think about who could be out there looking at them. Dan had been down there for some time and if they didn't work faster he would not make it. Things began going much better for them. The rope was past the thin spot and they could all pull at one time.

"One, two, three, PULL!"

"One, two, three, PULL!"

"This is going well", the three of them were thinking.

But Dan was not thinking it was going well. He hurt all over and by now he was sobbing softly to himself. He didn't want the kids to know. He knew they were doing the best they could, so, he just hugged the rope and kept his head down so that they would not see him cry. He began trying to help. If he saw a spot he could grab, he would. It didn't do much good but he felt better doing something.

A rock came crashing down just next to Dan's head. The rope had cut it away from the edge. Nick, Beth and Kim felt the rope jump in their hands but didn't know why. They stopped. Kim ran to the edge to see if Dan was okay.

"What was that?" she asked.

"A rock came down just by my head," said Dan. "But, I'm okay. It smashed over there into the bushes. So, let's keep working. We're getting there."

"We better not go too fast," Kim said. She picked up her part of the rope and told Nick and Kim about the rock.

"I didn't think of that," said Nick. "It could have killed him. Did he look okay to you?"

"He didn't look up at me so I don't know if he is. Let's just get him up here before things get bad. He can't be doing well if he wouldn't look at me."

The rope came over the rock little by little and with Dan's help it was not too bad. When he pulled himself up with the rope it was a lot faster.

"He must be getting to the top by now," Beth said softly. "Can one of you look?"

"Okay, I will," Kim said, "but don't let go of the rope."

Kim looked over the edge. Dan was still hugging the rope but he did not look up or say a thing when Kim asked how he was.

"Dan! Dan!" she yelled. Dan still did not look up.

"Oh, no!" she said to Beth and Nick. "I think he has passed out but is still hugging the rope.

One or two more and I think we can get him over the edge. Let's do it! Let's do it now!"

She grabbed the rope and they all did their best to get Dan to the edge. Nick grabbed Dan as the girls kept the rope around the tree. At last they got him over the edge. He just lay there. Nick took the rope from Dan's feet. He and the girls sat down next to Dan not knowing what to do next.

Chapter

Five

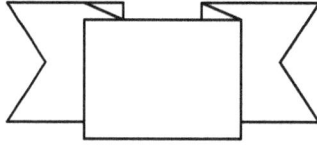

Bob went back to the camp. He thought that the rest of the kids should be back by now. When they weren't there he was upset. He didn't know how Dan was and he didn't know if that man had come after them.

Who was that man? Could it have been the hermit that folks have talked about? He could be anywhere and Bob would not know it. There were a lot of spots that he could be right now just watching.

Bob began to think back about what had happened. Why did the man get so upset when all Bob wanted was for him to help Dan? Come to think of it, the man hadn't even tried to find out what Bob wanted. Bob remembered that when he got to the water he had just yelled "Hi".

****

The man that the folks called "The Hermit" jumped up with the fishing rod in his hand when he heard the kid yell. He did not know what to think. No one ever came to this part of the lake. Was someone out to get him again? How did the kid get out here and what did he want?

****

When the man didn't yell back, Bob thought that maybe he hadn't seen him. Bob kept working his way over the rocks and down to the lake so that he didn't have to yell at him. Bob waved to him but "The Hermit" didn't wave back. That should have made Bob stop and think, but he didn't. He just kept working his way down.

Bob remembered that as he was making his way to the man he kept talking. "How is the fishing here? Did you get some? I wish I had a rod. I like fishing. My Dad and I go fishing a lot, but we don't come out here."

****

By now, the hermit began getting away from the water. He was thinking, "Maybe I should just get out of here. Maybe the kid wanted trouble. Well, I'll let him come over. Then he'll find trouble."

The man waved the fishing rod at Bob and began yelling.

****

This took Bob by surprise. He stopped and looked at the man running at him. The fishing rod waving and the yelling made Bob think back to what had been said. "A Hermit made his home in the bush." No one had seen him but the kids had been told about him.

Bob was thinking, "This must be him. He looks like a mad man. I have to get out of here. He's crazy." He wanted to run but his feet felt like he could not get them going. His head was saying, "Run! Get out of here!" but his feet would not do what his head was telling him.

At last, his feet let go and he began running. He looked back and saw that the crazy man was still coming after him. He fell over a rock but got up and kept going. He was fast on his feet but so was the man. He was getting winded but knew he could not stop if the hermit didn't stop. He could not take time looking back now because that would give the man time to get up to him. So, he kept running faster and faster. His ribs hurt because he was so winded but he kept at it. He tripped again and fell. Now, he just lay there. The man must have stopped. Bob could not see him now, so he just lay there thinking.

"The HERMIT, what do I know about the Hermit?" He began thinking of all the things he had been told. There wasn't much, because no one knew much. The Hermit had not hurt anyone. So maybe that wasn't the Hermit who was after him.

The Hermit could not fit in when he came back from the war, Bob remembered. He must not like anyone. "Is that why he ran after me?"

Bob asked himself. "Is that crazy man the Hermit?"

At last, Bob felt rested and his ribs didn't hurt. He got up and began making his way back to the camp. He was so upset that he took his time getting back. He was asking himself if he should tell the rest of the kids about the man. If he told them maybe they would want to get out of the bush and it would end their camping trip. But if he didn't let them know, and someone got hurt, he would feel badly. He didn't want anyone getting hurt.

Bob got to the camp and went right to his tent to get some food. When he went into the tent, he began looking around. Things were not where he and Dan had left them. Well, maybe the kids had come back to camp when he had been down by the lake. That must be it. The rest of them came back for food and left again.

Bob grabbed some food and went back out. Now, he felt like he did not want to be by himself any more. He began picking up some wood for the fire. All the wood that they had was going to be for the fire because they would want a big fire for the end of the day.

****

The man that folks called "The Hermit" had run Bob off and headed back to the lake. He was feeling badly that he couldn't help the kid, so he picked up his things and went back to his house in the bush. He knew that he couldn't have kids running around out here. This was his spot to be by himself. It had taken him a long time to find this spot. He knew that he would not hurt anyone, but he also knew that he could not begin over again looking for another spot. He knew that kids could make big trouble for him. It had happened to him before and he didn't want it to happen again.

"I just hope that I got rid of him once and for all," he was thinking. "If I must I will upset him even more next time."

But soon the man began feeling badly again. A boy had been hurt and he could have helped but he didn't. What if the kid just wanted to make trouble? I wish I knew what to do.

****

"What was keeping them?" Bob asked himself? "Did they have trouble with the Hermit, too? Maybe they could not get Dan up or down off the rocks and the Hermit had gone after them. He was by himself but they had each other so they should be okay."

He lit the fire. Maybe if they smelled the smoke, they would come back to camp looking for him.

Chapter Six

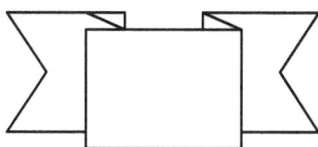

Bob thought he had trouble, but the rest of the kids had much more trouble than he had.

They were feeling better once they saw that Dan had not been badly hurt. As he lay on the ground beside them, the kids knew that he would be okay. The blood was coming back to his skin and he was looking much better. His one leg began kicking just a little. Then he surprised them by getting up and looking around.

"Where am I?" he asked.

Then he knew that he had passed out and somehow the others had dragged him up and over the edge of the rocks.

"I feel so badly about all of this. The edge of the rock cut away and must have hit me. Should we go back to camp and put something on my hand? Or, I could go back and all of you could go have some fun. I'll find you after I do that, okay?"

Beth, Kim and Nick just sat looking at   Dan. They were too surprised to know what to think.

"Is he all right or did he hit his head as well as hurt his hand? He is acting as if things are okay.

Does he know how bad things were for him? Is he just trying to make it up to us for the trouble he put us in?" Kim was thinking.

Kim got up and said, "Let's all go back to camp."

So they all headed back. They were quiet as they went.   They picked up wood for the fire just because they wanted to do something on the way.

After some time had passed, Beth asked, "Do you smell smoke?"

Kim said, "Yeah, I think I do. Do you think Bob is back at camp?"

At that thought, they went faster to get back and see if Bob was there and if he was okay. The wood fire was giving off a lot of smoke as they got to the camp.

"Did you have to make that fire so big?" asked Nick as he saw Bob working on it.

"I was trying to get you to come back to camp. So yes, I had to make it this big because I didn't know where you were," Bob said. "Are things okay?"

"We could have had trouble but yeah, we're okay," said Kim. With that, the kids all sat by the fire thinking of all the things that went badly. Dan went to his tent to put something on his hand. When he came back he asked, "What can we do next?"

"Are you crazy?" asked Nick. "Don't you think you should just rest a bit?"

"No, I'm not crazy. Let's get going. We can't just sit here. Let's do something!"

With that coming from Dan they all felt better and began putting the fire out.

"Where to?" asked Bob.

"We've been that way, so let's head into the woods this way. We don't know what we will find, but it could be fun. There is no path this way so maybe we'll see something that no one has seen before. There is no path so we will have to make one."

"Maybe we should have some food. I know I want something," said Kim.

After they ate, they put the rest of the food away. As they did this Bob asked, "Didn't you come back for food when I was down by the lake?"

Nick said, "It took us all that time to get Dan up off the rocks. I came back for rope but other than that, we have not been back. Whatever made you think we were here?"

Bob told them that things were not in the spots that they had left them. The kids knew that Bob was upset about something. Maybe he was just making this up but, they knew too, that Bob did not make things like this up.

"Bob, when I came back to camp for rope I left things where they were. Maybe you just put things in your tent that way when you got here."

Nick said. He was getting a little jumpy at the thought that someone may have been in the camp when they were not there. No one was around that they had seen. Bob wanted to tell them about the Hermit, but not now.

"Okay, maybe I did move things but, I don't think so," said Bob. "So, let's just get going." But Bob knew that someone had been in the camp and now he knew that it hadn't been the rest of the kids. So who? The Hermit? "This is crazy," he was thinking. "But, I had better just let it go for now."

They went into the bush but could not find a thing. So, they headed back to the camp. They were being bitten by bugs and that didn't help.

"Well, what now?" asked Kim. "This is not the best camping trip I've ever had!"

"Anyone up for fishing?" asked Dan.

Bob didn't want to go to the lake but he couldn't tell them that. No one had a better thought, so they grabbed their rods and headed to the lake.

They picked out what looked like a good spot and sat or lay on rocks in the sun. This was just what they all wanted after what had happened. No one said much. They were all looking at the water, thinking their thoughts and liking the quiet.

Dusk came before they knew it.

"We'd better get back to camp," said Kim. "I don't know about the rest of you, but I want some food. I thought we might get some fish but since that didn't happen, it's a good thing we have food at the camp."

"That was better than I thought it would be." Beth said. "I have never fished before. I think I like it. I don't know what I'd do if I got one. You would have to stop me from yelling as I ran all the way back to my house!"

They were all laughing as they got back to the camp. But when they got there the laughing died.

Things at the camp were all over. It was not a mess but things that were in the tents were now out by the fire. Their firewood was not where they left it.

Who had been there and WHY?

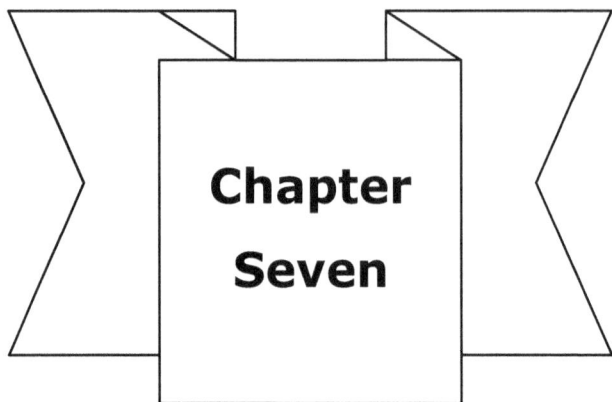

Chapter Seven

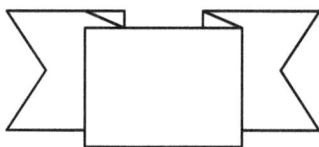

As they picked things up and put them away they felt as if someone could be watching them. They kept looking around but could see nothing or no one in the bushes or on the rocks. They were quiet as they put things back into their tents. When nothing happened by the time they had things put away, they began to feel a little better.

"Maybe we should pack up and go home." Kim said as she came out of the tent. "There was someone here. When Bob said that someone had been here before, I didn't want to believe him. Now we know that someone is out there. When we are not here, they come and mess with our stuff."

"Think about it," said Kim. "Nick, you said that someone was here after we went to sleep last night. Bob did find his things were not where he left them and now, this! Let's get out of here BEFORE we find out who this someone is."

"If it wasn't dusk and we had time to pack up all this stuff, I would like to get out of here, too," Nick said. "But, I don't think we could get things packed and back home. I say we stick it out here. What do you think, Beth? I know this stuff must be upsetting you if it is getting to the rest of us."

Beth was sitting on a rock by the girls' tent. She had not helped put things away when they got back to camp. She just sat down and let the others put things back. The rest of the kids knew that Beth would be more upset than they were, so they let her be. Now, they wanted to see if she would be okay if they didn't go home.

At last Beth said, "I think Nick did see someone last night AND someone in the bush when we were getting Dan off the rocks and now we all know that someone was here. But, let's think about it. We cannot make it home now. We have to camp here for one more night. I don't like it, but we are trapped here for now."

The rest of the kids knew that she was right. Not saying a thing for a long time they just sat there by the fire pit.

The sky had become black, so Dan lit the fire to get it going again. Dan began getting some of the food from a tent and at last, the others got up and did the same. They all wanted to eat and that made them stop thinking of the spot they were in for now. They felt a little better after eating something. They made the fire bigger. They sat and looked at it, not saying much.

Then Bob said, "Why are we here? We came to have a good time. Let's not let this stop us from having fun. So, someone came into the camp. They came when we were not here. They were just looking for something. They didn't take a thing. They didn't come when we were here, so they are not out to get us or hurt us."

"Yeah," said Dan. "Why are we so upset and letting it stop us from having a good time? There are five of us and only one of them. So, I think we are okay. Let's tell some funny stories and not think about all that now. I bet I can get you all laughing when I tell you what my dad did the other day."

As Dan told the story the kids began to laugh. Dan was good at taking a little story and making it into something that was very, very, funny.

It did not take long and the others felt much better. They began telling stories about their dads or their moms. Back home they did not get to tell stories about their folks. But now, sitting by the fire, they found it was great fun. They added things to the stories that made the kids laugh even more. They knew one another's folks, so that made the stories funnier. They were laughing and kidding and time went by so fast that they could not believe it. The girls got some food from their tent and things were just as they had wanted them to be – sitting by a campfire, laughing and kidding and telling stories.

After a long time the wind began to pick up. They did not know what time it was and they did not want to stop the fun and go to bed. The kidding and laughing slowly came to an end and they knew that they should put the fire out and get some sleep.

"Well, I think it's time," said Kim. "Will you be okay if Beth and I go to bed now?"

"What do you think boys?" Dan asked Bob and Nick. "We are just great. Things are good. We know that no one is after us and there are five of us. Just yell out if something happens but I don't think it will, so go get some sleep!"

As the boys were putting the fire out, Bob told them about the Hermit he had seen down by the lake.

"He got mad and came after me. All I wanted was to ask him if he could help us get Dan down. Maybe HE came to the camp. Maybe HE was the one who was here in the night and then came back when he knew we weren't here. He could be in the bush watching us right now. I know we can't stay up, but what should we do? That man seemed a little crazy to me. He is the only one out here that could have come to the

camp. Do you feel like someone is watching us

right now?"

Chapter Eight

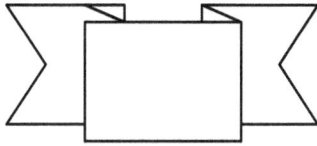

The fire was going out as the boys went to their tents to get some sleep. After all the things that had happened that day, they could not stay up. As they went by the girls' tent, they stopped to see if anyone was talking in there. All was quiet, so they knew that Kim and Beth were asleep. They made their way into their tents and were asleep in no time.

The sun was beginning to come up when Bob sat up. "What was that?"

He sat quietly. He didn't want to get the others up if nothing was out there. He had slept so well that he thought maybe he was just on edge. After a long time, he lay back down but could not go back to sleep.

It was still dark and everyone but Bob was sleeping. In the blackness someone hit the side of the girl's tent. They began yelling and yelling and yelling. In a flash the boys were at the girl's tent.

"What?" Nick yelled. "Why are you yelling? What happened?"

"Someone hit our tent." Beth yelled. "We are not making this up. Someone was outside our tent."

By this time the sun was up and as the boys looked at the tent, they could tell that it was not upright.

"This is the time to tell the girls about the man running after me and who I think he is," thought Bob.

When Bob told them all about it, the kids remembered what they, too, had heard about the man living in the bush. After talking some more they believed that all of the things happening must be the work of the Hermit.

Since it was their last day for camping, they all thought it best to eat, pack and just go home. They had planned on staying for the day, but now they just wanted the trip to be over. Bob didn't tell them about what had happened when it was still dark, but he did want to take a look around. As the others were getting the food, he went to the edge of the bush. He could see a man's tracks going into the bush and coming out again. There was more than one set of tracks and so he thought, "Was there just one man who came and went or was there more than one. It's just as well that we are getting out of here. We are all on edge and we wouldn't have any fun anyway."

"This was not the camping trip I thought we would have," said Nick, as they were packing up.

"You can say that again," Dan said. "I like camping a lot, but I don't know if I am going to like it as much any more!"

By noon they were all packed. They put mud on the fire pit and looked around. They had not left anything and so they headed for home.

"Our folks are not going to believe that we came home at noon from a camping trip. Are we going to tell them about why we are back?" asked Kim.

"I think we better. They may want to do something about that Hermit. If someone camps out there, it could be bad. As I said, there were five of us and so we were okay," said Dan. "I don't know what I would have done if I had been by myself."

"Our folks can't get upset with us for this one. The trouble was not because of something we did this time," Kim said.

As they got back to their block they felt less on edge. They wanted to get home and let their folks know about the Hermit. They wanted to find out what they would do about him.

Nick could not believe that his folks were not surprised to see him home at this time. The other kids were surprised, too, that their folks didn't ask why they were back so soon. Their folks did ask about the trip, but didn't ask about any trouble.

After a long time Nick asked, "Aren't you going to ask if we had any trouble?"

"Why?" said Nick's dad. "We didn't think you'd have much trouble on a camping trip. Did you?"

As Nick was telling his folks the story of the trouble they had and the hermit they saw, the rest of the kids were telling their folks the story also. Their folks didn't seem to be upset. All they said was, "You kids must have taken the hermit by surprise. He knows that no one goes out there."

"Aren't you going to do something about him?" Dan asked his dad.

"That man is crazy," Bob told his mom and dad.

All Bob's dad said was, "He did run after you but if he had wanted to hurt you, he would not have stopped. I think he just wanted to scare you off."

"I think you should do something about him," Bob said a little upset.

The kids' folks told everyone they should go over to Beth's house and see what her mom thought should be done. The kids knew that Beth's mom was a cop and she should know what they could do – if anything.

The kids and their folks all got to Beth's house at about the same time, as if it had been planned that way.

"Now," said Beth's mom, "Tell me what this is all about. What happened out there that made you kids so upset and made you come home before you had to?"

The kids told the story about what they had done on the trip. They left out that Dan had gotten himself in big trouble. When they were telling about things being upset at the camp, they could not believe that their folks just sat there.

Their folks didn't even seem to get upset at all that someone had bumped into the girls' tent in the night.

When they stopped telling the story, their folks just looked at each other and laughed. Then they laughed some more and kept on laughing and laughing until some of the moms were crying from laughing so much. The kids were stunned. That's when Beth's mom said to the others, "We did it! We gave them a camping trip they will NEVER forget!"

The Hermit

The Hermit liked where he had his home. He liked it here because no one came here. That came to an end when some kids set up camp. Now he must get rid of them. He would do what he could to make them get out and not come back.

Of all the spots the kids had looked at for their camping trip, they picked this one. They did not know that the hermit's house was in this bush until things began to happen.

"Five friends sticking together no matter what happens! That's true friendship!"

Linda (teacher)

"I kept waiting to find out what the hermit would do."

Russell – age 27 Adult Learning Centre